"There is such pain and understanding of our condition in Jeremy Halinen's poems that at times it becomes almost unbearable. But it is all justified in their diamond-cut depth and (paradoxically) clear density, as when the poet and we are 'both sides of the coin at once: / heads, laughter, and tails, tears.' Halinen's is a powerful and original, insistent voice. This is a strong book and full of courage."

Ronald H. Bayes, author of *The Casketmaker*

"'Just as some songs are desperate to be sung,' these words have begged to be written and to be read and read again... to 'transcend the universe of not.' Jeremy Halinen has chosen, whether there were other choices or not, to listen and to let these words sing. The stars may 'stay where they are,' but I suspect that they, too, will be moved by this powerfully raw, yet tender, premiere."

Denver Butson, author of *Illegible Address*

"The poems I long for are the ones crawling into and out of the dark. Not answers. Something better. Jeremy Halinen's *What Other Choice* is what I have been searching for with you. 'The moment the hand first enters the sphincter / is one of transition....' Here is something to pivot with into transition. Here are the poems we need to grip the bars above, and below. I'm a big fan of Halinen's book! You will be too."

CAConrad, author of *The Book of Frank*

"*What Other Choice* is essentially one long poem: a mosaic of meditations on exactly that: having no choice but to be true to the self. That choice, in name only, comes with a price, one that manifests like a bruise over many of these poems. Halinen utilizes a raw and sometimes violent lyric that seems to take the reader by force. And because these poems are never about the writing of the poems, they create a miraculous kind of sympathy, leaving us as bitter with experience and as mellow with acceptance and as much in love with love. Skillfully written, never overwritten, this collection is faithfully obsessed with its mission, dovetailing into a perfect mimesis of subject and style: the refusal to compromise one's truth."

Larissa Szporluk, author of *Embryos & Idiots*

"Here's a poet whose bravery sits just on the edge—a good spot!—of brashness. He's as tough on himself as he is on others. With ever the steely eye, his poems see the joys and triumphs, the scars and fresh scabs, of a life lived deliberately. A very strong first book of poems!"

Nance Van Winckel, author of *No Starling*

What Other Choice

Jeremy Halinen

Winner of the 2010 Exquisite Disarray First Book Poetry Contest

Selected by Kathleen Flenniken

Library of Congress Control Number: 2010939243

ISBN 978-0-9830448-0-2

Exquisite Disarray Publishing
Tacoma, WA
www.exquisitedisarray.org

 etisiuqx**D**isarray
www.exquisitedisarray.org

Exquisite Disarray Publishing is dedicated to highlighting the work of Northwest writers,
with a particular emphasis on writers who have not previously published a full-length
book. All proceeds from the sale of Exquisite Disarray books go to support this mission.
A nonprofit corporation registered with the State of Washington, Exquisite Disarray
recognizes that environmental sustainability and cultural sustainability are interdependent
and seeks to foster their mutual growth.

Exquisite Disarray Publishing is an Associated Program of Shunpike, a 501(c)(3)
nonprofit arts service organization that supports local arts communities by partnering
with small and mid-size arts groups. Shunpike provides support to Exquisite Disarray
Publishing in the form of financial reporting, organizational management, and arts
administration.

Cover and book design by Anne Halinen
Cover Art: Portion of *The Tomb of The Diver*, a ceiling fresco at the Southern Cemetery at
Paestum, Italy, c. 480-470 BC, artist unknown

Printed and bound in Washington State, USA
on post-consumer fiber recycled paper

The text of this book is composed in Adobe Caslon Pro with the display set in Lithos Pro
Composition is by Anne Halinen

for Ron Bayes and Nathan Whiting

CONTENTS

FOREWORD

Birthdays are strange affairs, intensely personal and banally universal: whether we observe them or not, everyone has one, and that includes small nonprofit presses. Still, I paused at this year's arrival of September 29 (a birthday shared by Cervantes, Elizabeth Gaskell, and Jerry Lee Lewis), recalling that day in 2008 when I filed the articles of incorporation for Exquisite Disarray Publishing. I learned later that I'd done everything backward, incorporating before I had a board of directors in place; fortunately, friends and colleagues were kind enough to sign onto the community poetry project that had been my inspiration. Titled *In Tahoma's Shadow: Poems from the City of Destiny*, the anthology that emerged offered a diverse view of the Tacoma poetry scene, from pastoral to post-industrial, from sonnet to spoken word.

Seeking to build upon the momentum of *In Tahoma's Shadow*, Exquisite Disarray's board embraced the idea of a first book contest, in which we would publish one winning poet. We decided to invite poets from all of Washington State to enter, as we felt that this would highlight Tacoma's role as a center for literary arts. When the submissions arrived, we knew that our decision to expand statewide had been the right one; we received manuscripts from Auburn to Leavenworth, from Seattle to Tacoma, and we were impressed by the overall quality. We read without preconceived criteria as to form, style, or subject matter; we were simply looking for the best poetry. In the end, we recommended nine manuscripts to our outside judge, Kathleen Flenniken, author of *Famous*, the winner of the Prairie Schooner Prize in Poetry, and coeditor and president of Floating Bridge Press. From those nine, we asked Kathleen to select the top three, and from those three, Jeremy Halinen's *What Other Choice* emerged as the winner that Exquisite Disarray would publish.

Kathleen deserves our gratitude for helping a young press such as Exquisite Disarray negotiate the challenges of the selection process, and we also thank her for her bravery in helping to choose as our winner a manuscript whose frank treatment of sexuality might have led a more timid judge to choose a less controversial book. And as I write, I note that we've just passed another significant birthday: on October 3, 1957, Allen Ginsberg's *Howl* was welcomed into the world of legally available poetry when San Francisco Municipal Judge Clayton W. Horn ruled in favor of free speech in publisher Lawrence Ferlinghetti's obscenity trial. "Would there be any freedom of press or speech if one must reduce his vocabulary to vapid innocuous euphemism?" Horn's decision asks, concluding that identity is both a speech act and a human right: "An author should be real in treating his subject and be allowed to express his thoughts and ideas in his own words." The enemy of vapid innocuous euphemism, poetry may or may not make things happen, but it steadfastly refuses to remain silent.

This refusal to remain silent takes many forms in Jeremy Halinen's poetry, from the gesture of evocative breath in "Rather Ordinary Skull" to the enunciation of a heartbreakingly impossible romance in "Dear Laramie, Dear Liar, Dear Once Upon a Time." In "A Brief History of Heavy Petting," one of several "brief histories" in *What Other Choice*, we see Halinen in the process of articulation—both a bringing into language and a literal "hinging"—as he constructs a mythology of first intimacy.

Or, as Halinen himself phrases it in "Some Nights Even God Is Agnostic," language can at times solicit us, can compel us to speak the words that "transcend the universe of not." Such compulsion may at times require that a poem speak uncomfortable truths, as many of Halinen's poems do; at other times, the compulsion to speech reveals uncanny beauty. It's that tension between the grit of experience and the grace of insight that engages us, that gives us promise, that keeps us reading. It's what brings me back again and again to lines from *What Other Choice* long after I think I've closed the book.

William Kupinse

By *disarray*,
I mean the look findable
in the eyes of a horse in storm,
and panicking.

                              Carl Phillips

ONE

No one calls on me
　　　but the wind.

　　　　　Antler

RATHER ORDINARY SKULL

I would say it
is empty, were it not

for the occasional
and vague

impression
it is perhaps haunted

by a moth
whose wings

cause a tenuous
wind.

A Brief History of Heavy Petting

It started in the cold, one boy
attempting to pay back another
a debt he thought he owed.

Intended only as a transfer
of heat, it listed soon
into the ark they'd been

waiting for. Deep in the cave
that night, far from the bark
of the moon, both knew it.

This was long before the dawn
of fiction, before their newfound
fortune could be called *trespass*

or *transgression.*
They are not alone.

AFTERNOONS ABOVE I-5

We used to drop acid
and sit on the overpass
to watch the dragon faces
the cars would make at us
as they raced
beneath our dangling legs.
Cars like it when you're high enough
above them to notice
more than their surfaces.
It's the story of their exhaust
they want you to care about,
not their paint jobs
or the treads
on their tires. They want you to lean down
and touch them.
I know what you're thinking.
It's dangerous,
what we used to do. But
the cars told us they'd catch us if we fell.
You say, *So what if they did?*
And you're right.
There's always a catch.

CLAIRVOYANT

I could say he glimpsed
in the distance my unbreakable
aura of joy

and, because he knew it was something
he could never possess,
wanted to break me

so it, though unbroken,
would go from me and
all humanity, all fauna

and flora, all memory
and dream, into the space
outside this planet,

a wandering cloak
with nothing to cover, but
when he drew closer,

he realized I was a man
made of water,
unbreakable in my liquid state,

unable also, because of my aura,
even if boiled, to evaporate,
so he invited me

into the deep freeze of his life
and waited.

SUGAR

1.

So many days I crawled to you
          for *I love you* or *I love you* with a hug
and, perhaps, a fuck, but hope
          is a home I can't live in.

2.

You were once a boy.

3.

You are a man.

4.

More, you say, *more.* This time, I don't resist;
          I let your fist wreck
what ship I have left, let it probe wrist-deep
          for the last life raft.

5.

          But something inside pulls it deeper,
refuses to let you use it.

6.

                    Old man, you
are losing everything. Even the ring
                    I put on your finger
is slipping. My sweet tooth
                    is under your pillow, silent;
not one life ring left.

PAUSE

I nailed your freshly severed
hands to the stop sign
at the end of our block.

Drivers stop long enough now,
as you always wanted,
for it to be called a stop sign.

You would be pleased
at your flesh demonstrating
how desire falls from the bone

when the brain is gone.
Though nailed hands
can't clap,

you would admire
how their bones crack
to let the marrow go.

FACING SECOND DEATH

You: ghost
on a scaffold,
words roped around your neck.
Snap, when the trapdoor drops, without
a sound.

WHERE THERE'S A FIST, THERE'S A WAY

Sometimes I think, *Now I know*, but
I probably don't. If I fuck, on average,
3,000 times a decade, should I be able
to recall each ejaculation? A police car can

be ejaculated on by many men and then
photographed, and the photograph
can be folded, the love note scratched into its surface
just before, bent. So I missed my ex-boyfriend's

funeral. I was busy fisting my current
boyfriend, his first time, if you must know.
The moment the hand first enters the sphincter
is one of transition, a non-energy-saving-

light-bulb-turning-on-at-the-entrance-to-the-tunnel
moment, like trying for years to prod a camel
through the eye of a funnel and finally
forcing it through, creating two very

personal eras, BF and AF, less a watershed
moment than a shitshed one, separating
the shits before from the shits after,
the old sheep you've suddenly forgotten

from the fascinating goats to come.

Two

But who would you be? asks the universe.
Not this. Not this body.

Larissa Szporluk

THE END OF TIME

After church, the older boys
chased me. I was all tongue and lifted
lips, thought they wanted to wrestle
me down and kiss me.
But they took my crutches
and ran off laughing.
One returned and muscled me down.
He sat on my chest
and, before I could get a hard-on,
lifted my head toward his
and smashed it down on the sidewalk
again and again, like an innocent cock
forced to try to rape the cold, hard ass
of a statue, the way death
itself is never the end
but always the means to it.

ESTRANGED

When he forces himself
        into me,
I feel feverish,
        moved within
by someone without
        who knew
my tongue could speak
        without my
bidding, against
        my will. Doesn't
she notice it's
        split, its contorted
flicker, my body's
        weird movement,
this slither? Today's
        forecast: regret
that one must know evil
        to recognize lies.

STRANGER

When I don the body
of the serpent, I see,
        for the first time,
the dawn and realize
        what a yawn it is
to be me: I AM THAT I AM—
        so what? To have every
perspective at once:
        as good as having
none. Goddamn this
        woman, this man
who see these trees
        from solid land alone.
I'll show them. Hey lady, taste
        the fruit of this tree.
You'll see, you'll see.

My Cock Is Climbing Mount Everest

It must have been something in
the cup of mushroom tea I drank,
something slippery like psilocybin,

or that when my closet's popcorn ceiling started
popping and dropped on me faster
than I could eat it I darted

out and bit the lavender head
off the broken-stemmed iris
you gave me instead.

Perhaps it was some queer poison
in the petals I didn't spit out in time
or a new look I saw in my irises' reflection

in the toilet. Baby, do you ever try to see
in that water how we got here?
Is it possible, do you think, for me

to be a girl as hard as glass
even though I have a cock
and like one up the ass?

I don't want to be Jesus of Fagareth any longer.
At 29, I have only four years left, and this time,
rather than use a cross and spear,

I fear they'll place my mouth
behind my forehead
and make me blow my queer out.

MY CITY

When I think of what I know about Spokane,
I think of beating my boyfriend's best friend
in the Safeway parking lot one evening,

between a Honda Accord and a cart return.
One moment making car talk, the next
my fist curving up to meet her

unsuspecting, smiling face. It was a sort of
violent surprise
that a bloody nose could turn me on

so much I'd almost wish I were straight enough
to take her home. Behind her
I could see the moon

rising slowly above Maple Street,
and I thought of my boyfriend, who always tries
to be good in every situation,

that such noble effort ought to be emulated.
Then I slammed my fist against her frown,
against all the time he'd thrown away on her.

My knuckles reveled in that moment, in the wetness
I'd always known she hid inside her.
When she fell to the asphalt below me

and tried to crawl away, begging
mercy, I bent and slapped her neck
until she asked me why. Then I wiped

my hands on her long brown hair
and went inside to shop. And who was left
to answer her? And who would know

what, or how, to say?

Dear Laramie, Dear Liar, Dear Once Upon a Time

Matt and I were walking hand
in hand down University Avenue,
sipping sweet tea in bright light
sent about eight minutes before
by the sun, nothings
slipping
now and again
from our lips,
which couldn't have been more
calm,
when two frat boys
approached us with lazy
grins on the faces
below the brims
of their hats.

We nodded at them
as we passed.

That night, we drove out of town,
parked at the edge of a field,
and made love awhile
by a split-rail fence
in light sent long before we were born
by some stars.

EARTH

From this disadvantage point, I point out
the gay gods' teeth planted in pathways
I will likely never walk with my hand
in the hand of another.
And what of the toothless gods? Do they ignore us,
their mouths full of what they traded their burning bones for?
We worship, but still we die at the hands of men
who hold hands with women
and guns.

THREE

I've dreamed of you so much that my arms, accustomed
to being crossed on my breast while hugging your shadow
would perhaps not bend to the shape of your body.

Robert Desnos

A Brief History of Disbelief

It's the other man's indifference, finally, that lifts
this man to his feet, less grief-stricken
than amazed his flirtation
failed. As he walks away across the bar and out
the door, he imagines the one he wants to want him
looks the other way. *It's just another hole*
to climb out of, he thinks, but it's not a hole,
it's a parachute, and though he doesn't know,
he's safe beneath it in gradual descent,
yet if you say so, he'll say no, that it's a hot air balloon
full of holes from rockets and he's a basketed
basket case in freefall. But who's to say
the one who stayed *didn't* watch him leave,
doesn't want him, after all, tanned
and deboned, above his mantel awhile
for visitors to admire?

Inside the bar, no hot air balloons hover
in harm's way above sidewalks lined
with launch pads and trees, no leaves
turn slightly as the bartender passes
from one end of the bar to the other
and stands somewhere between the men.
He pours a gin and tonic,
rings it up, and feeds the till.
You drink your drink. As usual,
you don't know what to say.
Outside, the air is unusually still.

A BRIEF HISTORY OF TOUCH

The man beside me
in the bed said
he loved me, but
I didn't believe him
until he let me
fuck the hole in
his side.

BUGGERING YOU UNDER AN APPLE TREE

how like an inflated
earth
you are
apple
of my why
and i
globe of airplanes cars
and throwing
stars passing in and in
your handsome
gate
am hardly planet yet enough
to bear your skinsoft weight

THE WRIST OF LOVE

Though sought, no respite—
even in the midst

(inside you: him; you
inside him) of love—

from that hinge
so integral to us

we forget its name
is often desire.

At its farthest border
gestures what we've made

to grasp with, which,
if you'll forgive me,

I'll call, simply, the hand
of love, its fingers long

and slender, their callous tips
the closest we expect to get

to one another, not unlike
the lamb who,

despite his bravado,
when he lies down,

finally, with the lion,
has never been

more tender.

ELE—GEE

You left home and died,
and all I could
was think you were a *diar*:
an unfinished diary
or a liar
with a *d*-formed *l*.

That, and of Medusa's sisters:
unsightly, yes,
but always alive,
spooking to stone
even reflections
of their shadows.

From the laundry room:
muffled roar of the dryer.
And here, me not beside you, holding my hand
in deathbed-less why, unable
to laugh
you goodbye.

CHANCE

I was crossing Division, tossed
like a quarter and thinking of death,
when a giraffe
stilted past me toward the morgue,
where I'd just left you. *Impossible*,
I thought; I was nowhere near the zoo.
But the sight of that giraffe,
orange-black, off-white, and tall,
caught me, perpendicular,

tight in an invisible fist—
I was both sides of the coin at once:
heads, laughter, and tails, tears.

LIKE A PERHAPS SLAP

across a tongue that
should sooner have
slipped back into its
cave, like a sudden
grave that could not
help but be dug and
filled, like a dozen
men who would be
roses, stems together,
in a vase, if love
were easy to replace.

Four

What is vertigo? Fear of falling? Then why do we feel it
even when the observation tower comes equipped with
a sturdy handrail? No, vertigo is something other
than the fear of falling. It is the voice of the emptiness below us
which tempts and lures us, it is the desire to fall...

Milan Kundera

NOTE

Sometimes beneath me
buildings rise and I don't

want to jump.
I have lived longing for hard things,

so I welcome
buildings.   No one can tell me

the dying need doctors.
They need new bodies, and hardness

only buildings can bring.
If this building

were a magnet, this body
a magnet,

would you understand
why I was here?

I didn't jump.
The building disappeared.

WANTING HOURS

One can't bury a bird
that dies in flight
but flies on.

GHOST GUARD

lit like moon your face I know with its eyes
watches me sleep as I can't
but wish I could
watch
but oh
rock of mysterious
spirit oh frozen ocean of face
I see nothing through the smoke
when I wake
and light
the cigarette pupils of my eyes

RESURRECTION OF THE ANXIOUS EYE

In my fantasy about us, we lie,
facing each other,
on my double bed,

you on your left side,
me on my right,
one tear

drifting
from the corner of my right eye
to the white pillow case

and surprising me
because I hadn't known
I had a tear

left. You aim
your lips
at the damp spot

on the pillow case
and blow
till it's dry.

LIVING ROOM

If I had my way, I'd turn the TV off
and hold you, repeating *I love you I love you,*
but I don't.
I can't remember if I told you
I'd hold you when your time
to swim the Jordan came
and thus don't know
whether I broke another promise.
These days, I wear only one shoe.
I may have just one foot.

GRAND CANYON, SOUTH RIM

Someday some river
will sever our world in two

and gravity will be too frail
to hold the halves

together. We will be
on opposite sides, separate.

*

Rain that does not land,

*

An arc of spectral colors
will allow us

to together erase
distance, to race

as if one of us
could reach the other first.

*

Bodies preparing to fall,

*

We will clasp each other
until the colors under us

collapse
and after,

my eyes
nesting in yours.

*

Falling, swallowing the rain,

*

Untraceable as our shadow
sliding down stone.

Your eyes nesting in mine.

FIVE

For if I try to seize this self of which I feel sure,
if I try to define and to summarize it,
it is nothing but water slipping through my fingers.

Albert Camus

PUSHER

Say you're Sisyphus
and you want
to take a nap.

It's been millennia
since you've slept
or even had a lap

you could tempt
another man
to sit on.

You feel like a pawn
but smart enough
to know better.

You wonder if
you'd rather roll
an infinite

ball of yarn,
or polish the throne
of kingdom come.

Long ago,
you used to daydream
a man in shackles

standing chin-deep
in a stream
not of water

but of wine's stillborn son,
unconsciousness;
every time he leaned

to take a drink,
what he longed for
sank beneath his reach—

but now your thoughts
turn to waves
advancing toward,

then retreating from,
a too-familiar beach.

OR

Not so much my past
as a grasp on it

or, more accurate yet,
a path through it

from which to survey,
as in: There I am

on a stranger's
vomit-soiled sheets,

lost, no, cast
in alcohol-and-GHB-

induced sleep, still
unaware of what

he's done, blood
and shit and lubricant

and what he left
to mark, as if it

were his, the territory
still drying at

and around the selfsame
point of entry

and departure
as if his flesh

had been a hook,
barbed, that had been,

by me, caught,
as if my body

had been the trap,
the transparent net

lurking
in the fish's mouth,

and he'd been lucky—
and what other choice,

finally, did he have—
to tear free, an achievement

yielding, no doubt,
an elation stained

with sorrow
comparable to that felt—

at the unavoidable,
but for that, no less

stinging, loss
of six men—

by Odysseus
as he passed, safe

himself, through
Scylla and Charybdis,

unaware of his ship's
forthcoming wreck.

FRIGID

My stained teeth knocking
on the skin of your neck.

What's left of my head's
divining-rod hair

a standing ovation—
for joy, or just oblation?

Is this an end?
They always mention

resurrection, but do you really
want to return so thirsty

you'll discover again
and again your teeth,

twin rows of Moseses,
sunk in the parted flesh

of a loved one's neck,
her or his nectar rushing

your mouth's neutral shore?

HURT HART

Imagine a ship, from it
Mr. Crane
about to jump,
to follow a misspelling
of his first name
into the sea. This time
he has no bottle
of iodine to swallow—
from experience, he knows
that element
won't push him
off the end of the plank.

He'd rather, I imagine,
swallow a crewmember's
cum—I know I would—
than jump—don't do it,
Mr. Crane, don't do it—
so he hasn't
jumped yet,
perhaps thinking of
his breakfast with Peggy,
of the fun of
overeating
when you know you're about to die.

Scratch that. How
can you more
than imagine? What

if you land in a net?
Is he thinking of that?—
how it happened
before, how you think
you're almost home
but then you're back on board
writhing face-to-face
with a fish equally desperate
to jump.

BROMIDE

But there have been too many
answers—and none right. Thunder

seemed answer, lightning
question, but maybe both were both at once.

That so quickly
they could be, then could not, distressed you

but impressed me. We put paper bags
over our heads, walked barefoot

out into the storm. The bags yielded to rain
and plastered our faces.

We pressed holes in them to breathe.
I peeled mine off so I could see

and led you to the wheelbarrow full of water,
told you to lean over.

If pulp hadn't shielded them, your eyes
might have tried to answer rain-

and wind-troubled questions in their reflection
as I, in my way, *like lighting* I thought,

had my way.

Six

There is nothing I can do
but go on led by the flickering of a flame
I cannot name.

John Wieners

IN THE ALLEY

I was up against a dumpster, my hands
deep in his back pockets,
his tongue between my lips,
when I felt a dozen zeros
land in my heart, one after another,
as if someone small and invisible inside him
had carefully carved from each empty egg
in a tiny carton of despair
one oval slice of shell
and walked down the hall of my throat
and dropped them
without asking.

PREY

Just when you think it's time to sneak up and
pluck three letters from *despair*
and whisper something
sweet, to make it blossom, into the *ear* they make,
as if it really were something, this life
somehow pried from our false memory of going somewhere
before falling,

> the eye of a needle-thin passerby
> reflects a speck of light
> you suspect your eye's plank
> stole from the sun
> and sent, too soon
> or too late, his way.

POSITION

Perhaps I'd been dreaming airplanes in an age before airplanes
in which birds ruled the air with wing and song
and was therefore surprised when I woke in an unfamiliar field,
my anus bleeding into dry grass, an airplane passing above
like the ride from the bar to that ordinary field
and what happened there—in that space shadowed briefly
by the airplane—that can neither be remembered nor forgotten.

PERDIDO DESPUÉS DE LA TRADUCCIÓN

I was reading Neruda to you
over the phone
in your native tongue
when you asked if I knew
what a *flecha* was. An arrow, I answered,
after I glanced at its translation.

You were impressed until I told you
I'd misled you.
Then you asked me to define a word outside the poem:
¿Como se dice ventana *en Inglés?*
And I said: in English, *ventana* is the wind
blowing a *flecha*
through the letter o. You laughed
and asked me if I was high, though I wasn't.

Then, Sergio, you told me
you'd misled me too, that you
were as high as a *flecha*
passing through the tail of a kite.
And I laughed. *¿Recuerde?*
I had *risa* too.

SHORE STUDY

Half of me was hot,
half too cold. I had the numbers
of too many men in my cell
and didn't want to make one call. I slid
nearer to the bonfire
until my breath no longer whitened
the night air. I could hear
but not see the sea
and for once didn't want
to swim so far
I could never hear it again.

THE WALL STARING BACK

Why shouldn't I
give my computer
a hug?

*

At the club,
he was hard
even before
we started to dance.

*

The problem with
labyrinths
is not
that you can get
lost.

*

Far from this world
something I've always wanted
is moving farther.

SOME NIGHTS EVEN GOD IS AGNOSTIC

I found it in an empty box of toys.
What I mean is: when I emptied
the box of its toys, I found it
in its emptiness. I know no other way
to say this, so I'm waiting for the world
to make me new, suitable words.
Just as some songs are desperate to be sung,
so are some words to be spoken,
to transcend the universe of not.
An emptiness in my mind tonight
threatens to swallow the sky.
But the stars stay where they are.

NOTES

The epigraph to the book is from "Vow," a poem by Carl Phillips, which appears in his book *The Rest of Love* (Farrar, Straus and Giroux, 2004).

The epigraph to section one is from "Raising My Hand," a poem by Antler, which appears in his book *Last Words* (Ballantine, 1986).

The epigraph to section two is from "Mother of Days," a poem by Larissa Szporluk, which appears in her book *Dark Sky Question* (Beacon, 1998).

"My City" is after "My Country," a poem by Tony Hoagland, which appears in his book *Sweet Ruin* (University of Wisconsin, 1992).

The epigraph to section three is from "I've Dreamed of You So Much," a poem by Robert Desnos, which appears, in English translation from the French by William Kulik, in *The Voice of Robert Desnos: Selected Poems* (Sheep Meadow, 2004).

"The Wrist of Love" is for Carl Phillips; its title is after the title of his poem "The Rest of Love," which appears in his book *The Rest of Love* (Farrar, Straus and Giroux, 2004).

"Like a Perhaps Slap" is for Gregory Laynor.

The epigraph to section four is from *The Unbearable Lightness of Being* (Harper & Row, 1984), a novel by Milan Kundera, in English translation from the Czech by Michael Henry Heim.

"Note" is for Katherine Stribling.

The epigraph to section five is from "An Absurd Reasoning," an essay by Albert Camus in his book *The Myth of Sisyphus and Other Essays* (Vintage, 1991), in English translation from the French by Justin O'Brien.

The epigraph to section six is from section 5.8 of "A Series," a poem by John Wieners, which appears in his book *Ace of Pentacles* (James F. Carr & Robert A. Wilson, 1964).

Author's Acknowledgments

Grateful acknowledgment is made to the editors of the following
publications, in which these poems have appeared or will (some
in different versions): *American Poetry Journal*: "Bromide"; *Crowd*:
"Rather Ordinary Skull" and "Wanting Hours"; *Dos Passos Review*:
"Afternoons above I-5," "Chance," and "My City"; *EOAGH*: "Hurt
Hart" (as "Mr. Crane"), "Note," and "Position"; *Floating Bridge
Review*: "In the Alley"; *New Mexico Poetry Review*: "Some Nights
Even God Is Agnostic"; *Nexus*: "Afternoons above I-5"; *OCHO*:
"Buggering You under an Apple Tree" and "Dear Laramie, Dear Liar,
Dear Once Upon a Time"; *Poet Lore*: "A Brief History of Disbelief";
REAL: Regarding Arts & Letters: "A Brief History of Heavy Petting";
Scythe: "Resurrection of the Anxious Eye"; *White Crane*: "Afternoons
above I-5," "Buggering You under an Apple Tree," and "Note."

"Dear Laramie, Dear Liar, Dear Once Upon a Time" will also appear
in *A Face to Meet the Faces: An Anthology of Contemporary Persona
Poetry*, edited by Stacey Lynn Brown and Oliver de la Paz. "Earth"
first appeared in the anthology *I Go to the Ruined Place: Contemporary
Poems in Defense of Global Human Rights* (Lost Horse Press, 2010),
edited by Melissa Kwasny and Mandy Smoker. "The End of Time"
was chosen by the editors of *Palooka* as a finalist for the Palooka
People's Choice Award in 2010. "My City" also appeared in the
anthology *Best Gay Poetry 2008* (A Midsummer Night's Press/Lethe
Press, 2008), edited by Lawrence Schimel. "Perdido después de la
traducción" first appeared in *Pontoon: an anthology of Washington State
Poets, Number Ten* (Floating Bridge Press, 2008).

For their invaluable feedback on this book during its development,
my gratitude to Elizabeth J. Colen, Dana Guthrie Martin,
Christopher Howell, Gregory Laynor, Peter McNamara, Brett
Ortler, Amisha Patel, Lawrence Schimel, Katherine Stribling, and
Nathan Whiting—and for their feedback on particular poems in this
book, my gratitude to Sergio Barreda, Jeffery Beam, Bruce Beasley,

Beth Coyote, Jake Grossman, Carol Guess, Anne Halinen, Jonathan Johnson, Yusef Komunyakaa, José Kozer, Melissa Kwasny, Kimberly Lambright, Kristen McHenry, Jessica Moll, Kathryn Nuernberger, Shira Richman, Kristen Shaw, Nance Van Winckel, Maged Zaher, and Maya Jewell Zeller. My heartfelt thanks to the following (and to the above) for their encouragement and inspiration: Ronald H. Bayes, James Bertolino, Richard Blanco, Anita K. Boyle, Chrystalene Buhler, Denver Butson, CAConrad, Betsy Dendy, Mark Doty, Jim Elledge, Theodore Enslin, Clifton Garner, Edward M. Gomez, Kemp Gregory, Patricia Halinen, Jessica Halliday, Michele Harmeling, Brianna Herrera, Charles Jensen, Sema Krishna, Mark Lang, Joseph Massey, Thomas Meyer, Ron Mohring, Jean Monahan, Arnisson Andre Ortega, Carl Phillips, Travis Pope, Mary de Rachewiltz, Carlos Reyes, Debra Santelli, the late Reginald Shepherd, Kelli Ann Smith, Lynn Szabo, Marjorie Taishoff, Sam Valle, Dan Vera, Connie Walle, Emily Warn, the late Jonathan Williams, the late Keith Wilson, and Ted Wojtasik.

Thanks to Anne Halinen for her exquisite design and layout; I am ever in her debt.

Publisher's Acknowledgments

The book that you hold in your hands reflects the work of many individuals and organizations. In particular, we are grateful to the Tacoma Arts Commission for its steadfast support of Exquisite Disarray over the past two years, to the arts commissioners in general, and to Amy McBride and Naomi-Strom Avila in particular. We are fortunate to have the support of Shunpike as the arts service organization that handles much of our day-to-day business needs; to Ellen Whitlock Baker, Andy Fife, and the rest of the Shunpike team, our sincere thanks. We were lucky to have such a fine judge in Kathleen Flenniken, who showed sensitivity to both literary matters and matters of human sentiment. Brittany Short merits special mention for volunteering to administer manuscript submissions and facilitate our anonymous evaluation of each submission. We're particularly thankful to Maria Gudaitis, who generously donated her design of our First Book Contest logo, and to Leah Vendl for creating the Exquisite Disarray logo. We thank Adam Ydstie for his help in launching our Web site and updating it during the past two years. And, of course, we acknowledge our current board members Beverly Conner, Deborah Renee, Rosalind Bell, and Matt Jones, as well as our emeritus board members Hans Ostrom and Tammy Robacker.

Most of all, we want to acknowledge the creativity and dedication of every one of the poets who submitted manuscripts to Exquisite Disarray's first annual First Book Poetry Contest, including second-place winner Jean Musser, third-place winner Cynthia Neely, and Best Tacoma Poem winner Michael Magee. We could not have conducted a successful contest without the input of so many fine poets. We are grateful for every manuscript we received.

About the Author

Jeremy Halinen is a coeditor and cofounder of *Knockout Literary Magazine* (knockoutlit.org). His poems have appeared in *Best Gay Poetry 2008*, the *Los Angeles Review*, *Poet Lore*, *Sentence*, and elsewhere. He lives in Seattle.